I0137269

The Witch, the Elements and Magick: The guide for Wicca and Natural Magick: Natural Elements and the Witch

By Kristina Benson

The Witch, the Elements and Magick: The guide for Wicca and Natural Magick: Natural Elements and the Witch

978-1-60332-044-3

Copyright© 2008 Equity Press all rights reserved. No part of this publication may be reproduced, stored in a retrieval system, or transmitted in any form or by any means (electronic, mechanical, photocopying, recording or otherwise) without either the prior written permission of the publisher or a license permitting restricted copying in the United States or abroad.

The scanning, uploading and distribution of this book via the internet or via any other means without the permission of the publisher is illegal and punishable by law. Please purchase only authorized electronic editions, and do not participate in or encourage piracy of copyrighted materials.

The programs in this book have been included for instructional value only. They have been tested with care but are not guaranteed for any particular purpose. The publisher does not offer any warranties or representations does not accept any liabilities with respect to the programs.

Trademarks: All trademarks are the property of their respective owners. Equity Press is not associated with any product or vender mentioned in this book.

Printed in the United States of America

Table of Contents

When ever possible, hold the rites in sacred places such as forests, seashores, mountain tops, desert plains, or near a tranquil lake or river. If you can not do this, a garden or inner chamber is fine. Make sure that it is prepared in advance with fumes, flowers and ornamentation.   **170**

I. INTRODUCTION

WHAT IS NATURAL WICCA?

Some would say that the phrase "Natural Wicca" is tautology, as Wicca is inextricably linked to nature. It is religion that delights in the harmony and divinity in all that surrounds us, honoring the four elements and the spirit. Wicca finds divinity in the crystalline texture of a snowflake, the smell of a meadow after the rain, the sound of the ocean crashing on the sand. Witchcraft—a word often used interchangeably with Wicca-- is a spiritual system that thrives on the earth and nature.

The natural aspect of Wicca is humility in the face of nature, and seeking to tune in with the Lord and the Lady that are embodied every rock, tree, blade of grass, and animal. To practice natural Wicca is to seek a connection with the earth and all of her creatures, and to treat the fruits of the Earth as aspects of the divine. There are also similarities between Native American Shamanism and Wicca in that both revere nature, and honor nature and the spirits of the God and Goddess. Many Wiccans believe in a deity that is not definable, but still present in all living things. Others feel that everything in nature are true aspects of the Deity and it is not necessary to personify him or her as a Goddess, such as Athena, or, say, Demeter.

In any case, the reverence of nature and an interest in learning from the Earth and all she gives us is a crucial aspect of all forms of wicca, but particularly, Natural Wicca.

THE FIVE ELEMENTS

The most popular modern pagan symbol is the pentangle, a five-pointed star. This represents the power of the number five; the four natural elements of fire, earth, air and water plus the mystical fifth element of ether, or spirit. Wiccan tradition states that there are five elements. It is through these elements and their constituents that all things are created, and made to exist. Each of these elements are present in all things—even rocks, or petrified wood, for example.

These five elements should be integrated into your practice, and represented on your altar. The order and placement of the elements within your altar can be any way you like, but traditionally, it is based on the four cardinal points of the compass.

The two heavy elements are Earth and Water, and are Passives. The two light elements are Air and Fire, and they are Actives. Earth is the opposite of Air, and Fire is the opposite of Water.

There are also five elements of the human individual, which are: the mind, the heart, the soul, the body, and the essence.

Each of these five human elements is related to the five basic elements. The significance and application of these elements are woven into even the most basic of spells and rituals

WICCAN CELEBRATIONS & THE ELEMENTS

Wiccans celebrate 8 major rituals each year called "Sabbats". There are 4 major and 4 minor Sabbats. The major Sabbats include:

> Imbolc (February 2nd),
> Beltane (April 30th),
> Lughnasadh (August 1st)
> Samhain (October 31st),

while the minor Sabbats are:

> Ostara (Spring Equinox, March 21st),
> Litha (Summer Solstice, June 21st),
> Madon (Autumn Equinox, September 21st),
> Yule (Winter Solstice, December 21st).

The Sabbats are solar rituals marking the points of the sun's yearly cycle, and make up half of the Wiccan ritual year. The other half is made up with "Esbats", which are the Full Moon celebrations. There are 13 full moons each year which Wiccans take to symbolize the goddess.

A Sabbat, according to the church, is an assembly of witches that gather so as to renew vows to Satan. The word "sabbat" is a borrowed word, as it same root word as "sabbath", which is a biblical period of rest. Of course, witches and Wiccans in no way affirm loyalty to Satan. The Sabbats are solar festivals following the solar year, and so their mythology emphasizes the life cycle of the God. The God is associated with the sun, and the Goddess is associated with the moon.

The Sabbats' names and some of their purposes have been inspired by and taken from a variety of pagan holidays from a variety of cultures. The major Sabbats are loosely Celtic, while the minor Sabbats are Anglo, Saxon, and Norse. This may explain some of the duplication of significances between adjoining major and minor Sabbats.

Wiccans believe time is cyclical, and conceive the passing of time not in a line, but a circle. The circle is split into two halves for summer and winter, with the divisions occurring at Samhain and Beltaine. The two halves are ruled by a Light God and a Dark God, or by the Goddess and the God. The God rules winter, while the Goddess rules summer.

The Wheel, or circle, is composed of the four equinoxes and solstices as minor Sabbats, and the cross-quarter days as major Sabbats.

The Days referred to here begin strictly at midnight, and in the southern hemisphere, Sabbats are generally celebrated 6 months off from the traditional dates.

FOUR MAJOR SABBATS:

Samhain (sow' en)
15 degrees of Scorpio, or November 1

Wiccan mythology: The death of the God

Samhain is the Wiccan New Year and the Feast of the Dead. It serves to commemorate the dead, particularly those who have passed away recently, or who are particularly missed. Samhain is also a time for reflecting upon the last year, making plans for the upcoming one, and assessing the progress made on last year's goals.

It is only somewhat accurate to say that we start the year off by celebrating death. Another way to look at it is to acknowledge that Death is necessary for rebirth.

The Goddess enters her Dark phase as she mourns her son and consort, and the Dark God takes up the rulership of Winter, leading the Wild Hunt of the Fey upon the earth.

Imbolc (im' molc) or (im' bolc)
15 degrees of Aquarius, or February 1

Wiccan mythology: Goddess recovers from childbirth, becomes Maiden.

Imbolc is the beginning of Spring. The God continues to mature, as can be witnessed in the lengthening days, and celebrations frequently serve to honor light. The Crone Goddess of Winter transforms to the Maiden, who prepares the earth to begin its growth cycle once more. Imbolc is therefore also a holiday of purification. It was inspired by an Irish holiday dedicated to Brigid or Bride, goddess of creativity, smithing, and healing.

Beltaine

15 degrees of Taurus, or May 1

Wiccan mythology: marriage of the Goddess and God

Beltaine, the start of Summer, is the most important Sabbat after Samhain. It is a celebration of joy and life. Named for the Celtic fire god Bel, the lighting of fires is a ceremonial part of Beltaine events.

On Beltaine, the Light God has matured to the age of rulership and takes over from the Dark God. The pregnant Goddess turns from Maiden to Mother.

Lughnasadh **(loo' na sah) or (loon' sah)**

15 degrees of Leo, or August 1

Wiccan mythology: Aging God

Lughnasadh is the beginning of Autumn and was the time of the first harvest, and so this is a holiday of preparation for the oncoming winter, an to remind us of the God's impending death. The Goddess also enters her phase as Crone.

FOUR MINOR SABBATS:

Yule

Also know as Midwinter

Winter solstice (around December 22)

Wiccan mythology: The birth of the God

Yule is a celebration of life emerging from darkness and is honored with the exchange of presents. Evergreens, holly, ivy, wreaths, trees festooned with ornaments and decorations, and mistletoe can be symbolic of the God, still living and green in the dead of winter.

Eostara (os tar' a)

Vernal equinox (around March 22)

Wiccan mythology: Sexual union of the Goddess and God

Eostara (which later changed into the word "Easter") is a celebration of fertility, conception and regeneration. It is also a triumph of light over dark as from now until Litha days will be longer than the nights. Eostara is a time for cultivating the growth of ideas and souls, caring for our bodies and making sure we haven't forgotten the goals stated at the new year.

Litha

Also known as Midsummer

Summer solstice (around June 22)

Wiccan mythology: Apex of the God's life

This is holiday of transition, when the God transforms from young warrior to maturing sage. It is a time for rejoicing, but also of introspection, making sure plans are still on track and meditation.

Mabon

Autumnal equinox (around September 22)

Wiccan mythology: Decline of the God

Mabon was the second harvest, and is primarily a holiday of thanksgiving. It is also the day when the nights are longer than the days, and so it is a day of planning and reflection.

The relationship between the seasons, the elements, and even color will eventually become second nature to you. For now, it is important only that you recognize that the Sabbats and Celebrations are ways of acknowledging the cyclical nature of time, the seasons, the elements, and the Earth,.

II. THE COMPASS & THE ELEMENTS

North

This is the direction of the Element Earth and the Power of Body. In nature, it takes the instantiations of rocks, clay, sand, and soil. In connecting with this direction, pay attention to your physiological processes, to the sensations in your body, to your biological needs, and to your physical health. It is the direction that binds us to ourselves, our physical bodies, and the physical earth.

East

This is the direction of the Element Air and the mind. Its Nature forms are the winds, the atmosphere, and the breath. This is the dimension of logic and thinking. In connecting with this direction, pay attention to your thought processes, to your ability to reason, to your attitudes, and to your mental health. It is the direction that connects us with our thought processes, and our abilities with reasoning and logic.

South

This is the direction of the Element Fire and action. Its Nature forms are flames, lightning, and electricity. It is the dimension of behavior and action. In connecting with this direction, pay attention to your of activities, and what you really do with your life and your time. Focus on how well you prioritize play, exercise, work, or worship. It is the direction that connects us with the fruits of our thoughts and the abilities of our bodies.

West

This is the direction of the Element Water and the Power of Emotions. Its forms are oceans, lakes, streams, rivers, wells, springs, dew, precipitation, and fluids in the body. This is the dimension of feelings, of emotions. In connecting with this direction, pay attention to your moods, and the way you experience emotions. It is the direction that connects us with our priorities and our passions.

III. WORKING WITH THE ELEMENTS: EARTH MAGIC

Direction: North

Colors: Black, brown, and green

Elemental: Gnomes

Time of Day: Midnight

Season: Winter

Tools: Pentacle

Zodiac: Taurus, Virgo, Capricorn

Animals: Bulls, dogs, deer, cows, bison, and mice

Places: Caves, mountains, forests, tunnels, and deserts

WAND MAKING

One of the first ways in which you can begin working with Earth magick is to carefully select and make your own wand. A wand doesn't necessarily have to be made of wood, but many are. It is important to know what type of tree the wood came from, and the properties of the given tree. Below is a concise list of the properties of several trees oft-used in wand making. Of course, you are not limited to using these trees, but the list may help you narrow down some of your best choices.

ALDER (Alnus spp.) This tree is a water lover and though it is of the earth, it has some water energy. It is oily, and fire resistant, and thrives in moist climates. Alder indicates protection and oracular powers.

APPLE (Malus spp.) A dense, fine-grained, rosy-coloured wood that even smells sweet, like the fruit. The apple tree is associated with choice, and is referenced frequently in religious texts. In Norse myth, Idunna was the keeper of the 'apples of immortality' which kept the Gods young. In Greek mythology, a golden apple was used to sew discord amongst the goddesses. And of course, in Christian and Muslim lore, the apple was used as a symbol of temptation.

ASH (Fraxinus spp.) A strong, straight-grained wood. Ash can be used in spells requiring focus and strength of purpose, and can be seen as symboloic the linking of the inner and outer worlds.

BEECH (Fagus spp.) Beech wood is closely grained, and is an old species of tree. Beech can channel guidance from the past to gain insight. It has the ability to offer spiritual protection, and can help those who are often in need of centering.

BIRCH* (Betula spp.) This pale, fine-grained wood is associated with fertility and healing magic. Birch grows easily and is often the first type of tree to take root after a fire or natural disaster has decimated a forest or landscape. Birch is an incredibly useful tree –the inner bark can act as a pain reliever and the leaves can be used to treat arthritis. Birch is most useful for fertility and healing spells.

BLACKTHORN (Prunus spinosa) Blackthorn is a winter tree. It is black barked, with thorns. It thrives in minimal sunlight, and grows in dense thickets. Blackthorn has dark energy, but is good for those who have too much fire energy.

ELDER (Sambucus spp.) Elder is a very hardy tree that easily regrows damaged branches and can root rapidly from any part. In Norse mythology, the Goddess Freya chose the black elder as her home, and the tree is associated with her. Elder is symbolic of the cyclical nature of life, death, and rebirth.

ELM* (Ulmus spp.). Elm is often associated with Mother and Earth Goddesses, and was said to be the home of faeries. The wood is sturdy, and resistant to cracking or splitting. Elm adds stability and grounding to a spell.

FIR (Abies spp.) Fir is a very tall slender tree that responds quickly to both the sun and the cold. It grows on the highest parts of a slope, and is symbolic of knowing the big picture.

HAWTHORN (Crataegus oxyacantha) Hawthorn usually doesn't grow much bigger than a bush or shrub, and the wood burns at a very high temperature. Its leaves and blossoms can be used to create a tea to soothe anxiety, stimulate the appetite, and improve circulatory function. Hawthorn can be used for protection, love and marriage spells.

HAZEL (Corylus avallania) In Celtic tradition, the Salmon of Knowledge is said to eat the 9 nuts of poetic wisdom dropped into its sacred pool from the hazel tree growing beside itMagically, hazel wood is used to gain knowledge, wisdom and poetic inspiration.

HOLLY* (Ilex aquifolium) The wood from the Holly tree is pale with very fine grain. Holly is associated with death, and rebirth. Holly can be well used in magickal workings having to do with sleep or rest, and to ease the passage into the next world.

LARCH (Larix europaea) This tree actually sheds its needles in the winter, which is unique. The smoke from burning larch is said to ward off evil spirits. Larch may be well used in magickal workings that seek protection, and the exposure to visions. It is also excellent for use in divination.

MAPLE (Acer spp.) A very hard, pale, fine-grained wood. The trees are laden with sugar, and the sap produces many varieties of syrup. Maple can bring success and abundance.

White Oak* (Quercus alba) this solid, dark wood is useful for spells requiring strength and solidity.

Brown (English) Oak* (Quercus robur) Brown oak has a very earthy feel, and is extremely useful for grounding. The oak is frequently associated with Gods of thunder and lightening such as Zeus, Thor, and the Lithuanian God Perkunas. In general, oak can be used in spells for protection, strength, success and stability.

PINE (Pinus spp.) The Pine tree is an evergreen, and coniferous. Pine is useful in spells seeking to cleanse the spirit and soul, and symbolizes rebirth.

POPLAR (Populus spp.) The White Poplar has elements of water energy as it best grows in moist, estuarine environments. The poplar has a strong association with speech, language, and communication.

ROWAN (Sorbus aucuparia) The Rowan tree is useful for spells seeking aid and protection against enchantment. The berries have a tiny pentagram on them, which is the ancient symbol of protection. The Rowan tree indicates protection and control of the senses from enchantment and beguiling.

WILLOW (Salix babylonica) The willow, growing and thriving in moist climates, has much water energy. Willow bark contains Salicin which is used in the treatment of rheumatic fever and various damp diseases. The bark can be used as an analgesic. In western tradition it is a symbol of mourning and unlucky love. Willow indicates cycles, rhythms and the ebb and flux.

CHARGING YOUR WAND

Once you have selected your wand, it will need to be cleansed, and charged. You will note that water, earth, air, and fire energies will be a part of the consecration process, though wands are of the earth.

To consecrate your wand, select a spot that is special to you, preferably out doors. You will need dried sage to burn, a silver or porcelain bowl, and a white candle. Light the candle and pick up the wand, and say:

"I have chosen this wand. It will assist me in my work."

Visualize the wand being cleared of any negativity, especially if it been touched by others, or served another purpose. Continue till the wand feels clear to you. Now visualize positive energy flowing from you, down your arm, through your fingers, and into the wand to its very tip. Visualize strong waves of energy flowing through your body to the wand.

Say:

> *"In the names of the Goddess and God (or Athena and Apollo, or whichever names you wish), I bless and make sacred this wand. I charge this wand by the element of Earth."*

Point the wand towards the North, saying:

> *"May the powers of the Earth cleanse and fill the wand I have chosen."*

Pass the wand through the smoke of the smoldering sage and say:

> *"In the names of the Goddess and God (use any names you wish), I bless and make sacred this wand, tool of my craft. I charge this wand by the element Air."*

Point the wand to the East, saying:

> *"May the powers of the Air cleanse and fill the wand I have chosen."*

Pass the wand through the candle flame, saying:

> *"In the names of the Goddess and God (using any names), I bless and make sacred this wand, tool of my craft. I charge this wand by the element Fire."*

Point the wand to the South, saying:

> *"May the powers of Fire cleanse and fill the wand I have chosen."*

Sprinkle the wand with water, saying:

> *"In the names of the Goddess and God (using any names), I bless and make sacred this wand, tool of my craft. I charge this wand by the element Water."*

Point the wand to the West, saying:

> *"May the powers of water cleanse and fill the wand I have chosen."*

> *"This wand is now ready, being consecrated and charged to assist me in my work. So mote it be."*

Perform other workings if you wish, then close the circle.

MORE EARTH MAGIC: BASIC MAGICKAL HERBALISM

One of the best gifts the earth has given us is her plants. Herbs are the basis of many modern, western pharmaceuticals, and with a little research, you may find that you can give up many of your expensive, synthetic pills.

What follows is a concise list of herbs and their magickal properties.

I have used several books as references, including:

Cunningham's "Encyclopedia of Magical Herbs" ©1994, Llewellyn Publications

Silver Ravenwolf's "To Ride a Silver Broomstick" © 1993 Llewellyn Publications

Mrs. M. Grieve's "A Modern Herbal" ©1931, Harcourt Brace

"A Handbook of Native American Herbs" © 1992 Shambhala Publications,

Back to Eden © 1981 Mass Market Publications, and my own experience.

Though by no means exhaustive, this list should be enough to get you started in herbalism. Later, you may want to consult this list when designing your garden. Having and cultivating an herb garden is the pinnacle of working with earth energy. Your studies of herbal medicine may prompt you to treasure some herbs above others. Even if you do not have a yard, you can create a perfectly useful and acceptable little garden out of pots on windowsills and counters.

Use caution when ingesting any herbs. Just because the herbs are of the earth, and not synthetic, doesn't mean they won't affect you. I can assure you that they will. White willow bark, for instance, has been used in painkillers. Valerian root can have a valium-like effect. Peppermint can settle the stomach. A catnip potion will make you sleepy. A mugwort potion will stimulate menstrual flow and calm nerves. A St. John's Wort potion for protection will lift your mood. You should be aware of the medicinal properties of every herb you ingest and also, remember more is not necessarily better. Herbs are to be used with as much care as synthetic medication.

USES OF HERBS AND SAMPLE POTIONS

Potions are the fusing of earth magick and water magic. Water magick will be covered with some more detail later. I have put the potion section under Earth Magick because it deals inextricably with herbs, which are of the earth. Potions also use air and sky magic as they are often prepared during a selected lunar phase.

An infusion is a strong tea, often made with fruit instead of leaves. Lemon, orange peel, and apples can be made into infusions. To make them, simply soak the ingredients in water that you have brought to a boil. After you pour the hot water over the ingredients, cover the cup, and let it steep. You may drink the infusion, or even bathe with it.

Solar infusions are much like the infusions described above, except the tea is not boiled. Solar teas use fire and sky energies in addition to earth and water energies. For that reason, many regard solar teas as the best method of brewing. When making a solar tea, the ingredients are added to the water and placed in the sun until the tea becomes warm. It's good to work with the astrological signs here if possible, but good results can come even if you don't take astrology into account. Another twist on the infusion is to make a lunar infusion, in which the tea sits out under the moon. Choose the best moon signs and phases here.

A decoction is like an infusion, but instead of dried fruit, it uses roots or other herbs with properties that are not easily extracted. Roots, seeds, and stems make good decoctions. Begin with cold water, and add the toughest roots first. Bring to a boil and simmer for about 30 minutes covered. Then let the mixture cool completely. If adding leaves or dried herbs to a decoction, you can take the decoction off the stove and steep your less hardy ingredients as you would an infusion. Be sure to cover throughout the process so the essence of the ingredients don't float away in the steam. When it's done, strain, and use the result.

Tinctures are another type of concoction you can make from herbs and plants. These are very good for homeopathic medicine, and I recommend consulting the book Back to Eden for a suggested list of useful plants. Tinctures are also good if you want to be able to store what you make, as tinctures contain alcohol. To make one, get a mason jar with a tight lid, and fill it with 4 oz. of herb and 8 oz. of alcohol—edible alcohol such as brandy or vodka, of course, if you plan on ingesting it. Seal the jar and keep it out of sunlight, at room temperature, for two weeks. For best results, initiate this process on the new moon and finish on the full moon. Be sure to swish the herbs around in the jar daily. When you finally open it, strain the mixture and store the result in an amber or blue colored bottle so it will not be degraded by sunlight.

A wash is a weak tea or infusion that is used externally, for bathing, for anointing, or for homeopathic practices.

A mild wash of 1/4oz. herb to one pint boiling water -- can be used to clean magickal tools, crystals, or talismans. You can even put it in a spray bottle if you'd like to spray the wash on, say, your altar, or other objects in your home. If you don't want to use a spray bottle, however, dip a leafy tree branch in the wash and shake the droplets out.

To make an ointment or balm, simply melt vegetable shortening or Crisco into a liquid form over medium heat. Add your herbs (one part herbs to three parts Crisco or lard or whatever) cover, and let simmer for about ten minutes. Strain out the herbs and store the remaining liquid in an airtight jar. This is for external use, and are not only perfect for Magick, but can be packaged prettily and sold or given as gifts.

Perfumes are made by blending essential oils together to create a fragrance. Choose essential oils and then add them to 1/4 cup rubbing alcohol, 1/4 cup witch hazel tincture, and 1/2 cup water. Shake it up, and you have perfume. As you get more experienced, you'll learn how to blend the oils so that the "notes" come out properly. Vanilla, for instance, makes a good top note and patchouli can make an excellent base. One of my favorite fragrances is a mix of amber, vanilla, and patchouli.

Oils can, of course, be expensive, but with a little practice, you can make them at home. Crush your herbs or flower petals and put them in a jar. Pour warmed safflower, olive, grapeseed, or almond oil on the herbs and steep for 48 hours in sunlight. Strain and repeat, adding fresh herbs. Do this as many times as necessary—some lightly scented flowers will require a lot of repetitions, so be patient. Store the result in dark bottles, away from sunlight.

For those who have little patience, time, or confidence to make their own oils and tinctures, flower essences are very powerful and can be made with little time or energy. These simple potions work on energetic and psychic levels. Pick a flower and place the petals in fresh spring water along with gems, crystals, and whatever other energies you'd like to add. Set the water in full sunlight for several hours. You can add brandy as a preservative. Again, these are great for ceremony, but also can be given as gifts or sold at farmer's markets.

Gem elixirs are made like flower essences, but by using crystals, rocks, and gems instead of flowers.

These are a few suggestions for making magickal potions to get you started, so you can peruse the list of herbs with purpose. You can make adjustments to the recipes all you like because the most important part of these potions is your Magickal energy. Enchant your herbs and charge your potions at the appropriate moon phases if it is not possible to create them at the ideal time.

LIST OF HERBS:

Ague Weed: a protection herb. Also called "Boneset".

Agrimony: acts as a deflective shield; sends back bad energy.

Angelica: highly protective. Can be used as an amulet.

Anise: Good for bringing about changes

in attitude, encouraging positive thinking.

Apple/Apple blossoms for love, peace, and contentment.

Ash Cleansing and purification

Asafetida: a very strong protective herb. Can be used to purify spaces that have been contaminated with bad energy.

Alfalfa: for financial success.

Allspice: works with other herbs to bring general good luck. Best as a booster with other herbs.

Althea: attracts good energy and good spirits.

Angelica: keeps away evil energy and evil spirits; can be used as an amulet.

Bergamot: sharpens the intuition.

Bistort: encourages material wealth.

Balm of Gilead: grounding and protective.

Barberry: used for hexing and dooming spaces to bitterness. As such, it should be used with great care.

Bayberry: casts a somber pall on the subject of any spell or tincture that uses Bayberry; encourages reflection.

Basil: for social success; encourages gregariousness.

Bay: induces prophetic dreams and visions; good for general luck and attraction of positive energy.

Benzoin: great to use as a booster, it magnifies the properties of other herbs.

Bergamot: protection and prosperity.

Betony: for removing negative energy; can be used to purify a space or object.

Blueberry: protective, particularly of bad energies.

Bindweed: used to dull the negative energies and intentions of others.

Bistort: fertility and sexual potency.

Broom Tops: purification and protection.

Black Snakeroot: an aphrodisiac and somewhat of a "love potion number 9"

Buchu leaves: used for psychic development

Cherry blossoms: bring honesty and encourages reflection.

Chamomile: soothes and calms nervousness and restlessness.

Caraway Seeds: protective; helps sharpen the memory.

Carnation: protection.

Camphor: to cleanse and sterilize.

Cardamom: a powerful love herb.

Clove: brings strength of will and resolve; excellent for blending with other herbs.

Cinnamon: an aphrodisiac. Cinnamon also helps prevent spikes in blood sugar, and can be a natural insecticide. Sprinkle on countertops or tabletops to get rid of ants.

Cedar: protection, purification.

Cherry Blossoms: associated with honesty and truth.

Capsicum (Cayenne): gives strength, resolve, and energy.

Coriander: used for love and friendship.

Citronella: for attraction. Good for attracting friends and business.

Cumin: can control impulses towards infidelity; encourages closeness and openness.

Calendula: induces prophetic dreams.

Dogbane: removes deception and dishonesty.

Deerstongue: acts to filter away bad energy and bad vibes.

Dill: for love and protection.

Devil's Bit: commanding and compelling.

Dragon's Blood: Power and protection.

Elder: highly protective.

Elecampane: for love charms of all kinds.

Eucalyptus: highly protective in areas of health. Also used for purification.

Elm bark: stops slander and general negativity.

Fennel: can remove hexes and create an unexpected turn of events.

Frankincense: associated with the male energies and acts as a sound "white" magical base to receive other herbs or oils.

Five Finger Grass: (cinquefoil) money spells.

Fenugreek: brings luck and success.

Frangipani: an attraction or

"magnetic" herb. Use to bring things to you.

Foxglove: exposes lying and deception.

Grains of Paradise: attracts good fortune and good luck.

Ginger: used to induce passion. A good catalyst to add to formulas for romantic love. Also can aid in digestion.

Geranium: used to lift the spirits and banish negativity. Can also be used in fertility potions.

Heliotrope: another sun herb. Attracts wealth and good spirits.

Honey: binds and attracts, seduces, charms.

Honeysuckle: best for rectifying

situations of infidelity.

Hawthorn: used for protection, purification and banishing.

Hazel: excellent for protection and to inspire others to trust you.

Hemlock: one of the foremost hexing agents. Added to any oil or incense to reverse its meaning.

Hyacinth: Attracts love, luck and brings peace of mind and restful sleep.

Heather: protects.

Hyssop: anointing, blessing, consecrating, purifying.

Irish moss: used to ensure success and growth in the long term.

Jasmine: essentially a seduction herb and aphrodisiac.

Juniper berries: a power herb which also acts as an aphrodisiac.

Lavender: cleanses, protects, can be used for uncrossing. Soothes and calms nerves, anxiety, and insomnia.

Lemon or Lemon blossoms: can used in love formulas to both repel and attract depending on the recipe.

Licorice: an aphrodisiac. Also aids in digestion.

Lemon Verbena: for luck, strengthening, and attracting.

Lemon Grass: is a good general power herb that can magnify the properties of other herbs when used correctly.

Lilac: brings peace and harmony. Is

excellent for reversing a hex; encourages peace and harmony.

Lobelia: to be used with the utmost care as it can be fatal if swallowed. As such, it poisons the effects of other herbs and can reverse them.

Lotus: associated with the magic of the ancients.

Lily of the Valley: used for calming and blessing.

Lime: To keep a lover faithful and to strengthen a relationship that is already in place.

Lovage: an "Attracting" herb. Does not need to be used just for romance; can be used to attract colleagues or friends.

Marjoram: protective - especially in matters of love. Can also protect the home and hearth.

Mint: peppermint is used as a stimulant and can give energy to the lethargic. Spearmint is calming. Both aid in digestion. Both aid in giving clarity and reason.

Mistletoe: for protection and to uncross a hex.

Myrtle: love, fertility, protection and healing.

Masterwort: power, strength and courage with good protective qualities. .

Mimosa: a commanding herb which also inspires deference in others.

Motherwort: a protecting herb.

Mugwort: clairvoyance, and the summoning of spirits.

Mullien: lends courage and helps troubles be laid to rest.

Neroli: (bitter orange) a magnetic oil used for attracting.

Orange or Orange Blossoms: attracting, drawing, can be used in love potions.

Orris: a focusing herb, used to focus the power of other herbs it is combined with. Also used as a "love herb"

Oakmoss: a power herb.

Patchouli: an herb of power and manifestation, for materializing one's wishes. Encourages sensuality and can act as an aphrodisiac.

Pennyroyal: Cleanses and protects. Brings harmony and is helpful in times of domestic unrest.

Peppermint: use to create change and

get things moving.

Pine: excellent for cleansing and uncrossing, protecting or refocusing. Energizing and grounding at the same time.

Poppy Seeds: for dreams, visions, and to induce a peaceful, relaxed states.

Queen of the Meadow: helps create new opportunities

Rose: general, nonspecific love. Can be mixed with other herbs for good results.

Rosemary: binds things (or people) together in a loving, gentle manner. Can also use for purification.

Rose Geranium: Reverses misfortune and can be used with other herbs to bless a new home.

Rue: highly protective. Often used in consecration rituals.

Sassafrass: Commanding and twisting.

Sandalwood: used to heighten spiritual vibrations, to cleanse, heal and protect.

Slippery Elm: a highly focused protection herb, especially against negative energy.

Snakeroot: can help you let go of a person, thing, or burdensome idea.

St. Johns wort: a quick-acting protection herb. Works quickly to reverse negativity.

Sweetpea: an attraction oil used to draw friends or lovers, loyalty and affection.

Solomon's Seal: an uncrossing herb associated with luck and wisdom. Brings hunches, intuition and dreams.

Strawberry: used to draw fortunate circumstances into one's life.

Squill root: very powerful for money

Thyme: encourages positive vibrations and actions.

Tormentil: (blood root) a commanding herb that can be used for good or ill.

Vanilla: a subtle seduction agent. Can also be used as a gentle aphrodisiac. Induces passion.

Vetivert: (khus khus) Excellent for uncrossing, protecting, cleansing and then refocusing.

Violet: for truth. Guards against deception and creates an atmosphere of trust and honesty.

ESSENTIAL OILS

Essential oils are derived from Herbs, and as such, are another part of Earth Magick. Though certain spells call for particular oils, you can use oils at your discretion to promote or capture a certain mood. Here is a list of oils and their corresponding properties.

To Aid Memory Recall, Sharpen the Mental State

Cedarwood, Marjoram, Peppermint, Rosemary

To Provide a Relaxing Atmosphere, Assist in Sleep

Chamomile, Clary Sage, Eucalyptus, Juniper Berry, Lavander, Mandarin, Marjoram, Neroli, Rose, Rose Geranium.

To Aid in Achieving Mental Alertness

Black Pepper, Cayenne Pepper, Grapefruit, Juniper Berry, Lemon, Peppermint, Pine, Rosemary, Ylang Ylang.

To Soothe Anxiety

Chamomile, Clary Sage, Eucalyptus, Juniper Berry, Lavender, Petitgrain, Rosemary, Sandalwood.

To Ease Conjestion

Eucalyptus, Ginger, Lavender, Lemon, Patchouli, Peppermint, Pepper, Pine, Rosemary.

To Relieve Physical Pain:

Chamomile, Ginger, Helichrysum, Lavender, Marjoram, Rosemary, Rose.

SOME USEFUL OILS

Oils, in my opinion, are an indispensable part of practicing Magick, much less necessary for a well-kept and pleasant home environment. They are, however, admittedly rather expensive. So here is a list of the oils that are the most useful, the least expensive, and the best to have on hand.

Lavender

Known to be calming, this oil is often used for insomnia. It makes an excellent addition to pillows, sachets, and baths. It's also good for general first aid, burns, and bites.

Tea Tree

This is an almost essential part of any first aid cabinet. The uses of Tea Tree oil are almost limitless. It is antibacterial, antiviral and antifungal, and be used to treat cuts, bites, dandruff, and athletes foot. It is extremely potent, but can be used without distillation or dilution. Care should be taken to keep it from children, and to be careful when using it on sensitive skin.

Eucalyptus

This is an excellent oil to have around for people who suffer from frequent colds, sinus problems, or congestion. Diffusing the scent can help break up congestion, and it is particularly effective when mixed with peppermint.

Peppermint

Peppermint can soothe headaches, act as a digestive aid, and ease travel sickness. Use in massage, a cold compress, in a diffuser, or as an inhalant. It also energizes, and reduces nausea.

Orange

Orange, or its more expensive counterparts of Bergamot and Mandarin, is uplifting.

Lemon

Lemon is great for cleaning, and studies have shown that a lemon-scented environment encourages others to be more diligent about cleaning up after themselves!

EARTH MAGICK WITH OILS & OINTMENTS

Priestess of the Moon Perfume

3 drops rose oil

3 drops vanilla oil

3 drops sandalwood oil

1 ounce grapeseed oil

Blend the oils in a bottle and shake to mix it. Ideally, the oils should be stored in a dark or amber bottle. This perfume is best used for the drawing down of the moon.

Earth Mother Perfume

Ingredients

patchouli oil
sandalwood oil
jasmine oil

Blend in equal parts, bottle and shake well.

Sun Energy Perfume

Ingredients:

Cinnamon Oil
Clove oil
Ylang-Ylang Oil
Black pepper Oil

Blend equal parts, bottle and shake well.

Perfumed Lavender Ointment

Ingredients

4 ounces beeswax
1⁄2 cup sweet almond oil
1 tablespoon Lavender essential oil

In a double boiler, combine the beeswax and the almond oil and let them
Remove from heat. Stir in the lavender and keep stirring for about a minute. Pour into containers and let cool completely until solid. When the ointment has cooled, use it as a perfume, and apply to the pulse points.

Rose Water

Ingredients:

1 cup distilled water

2 ½ tablespoons top shelf vodka, OR filtered well-quality vodka

20 drops rose fragrance oil

½ cup rose flowers (fresh or dried will do)

Tools

1 clean airtight container or jar

1 clean spoon

1 coffee filter or cheese cloth

1-2 airtight, amber or dark bottles to store the fragrance.

Fill the jar or container with the flower petals, and pour the water and vodka over the petals. Gently fold the petals into the water and vodka with a spoon. Add the essential oil and continue stirring.

Seal container and set in cool, dark place for one week, stirring every few days.

One week later, strain liquid through coffee filter or cheese cloth and discard the petals.

Bottle lavender water immediately. It can be stored in a dark bottle and kept up to one year.

Floral Perfume

2 tablespoons fresh rose petals

2 tablespoons fresh jasmine flowers

1 lemon peel, grated

1 tablespoon fresh Rosemary

1 tablespoon fresh Peppermint

2 cups water

1 1/4 cups vodka

Place the flowers, peel, and herbs in a small saucepan and cover with the water.

Simmer on low heat for 5 minutes but do not bring to a rolling boil. Cool completely and add the vodka.

Pour the mixture into a clean container with a tight-fitting lid and place in a cool, dry location for 2 weeks.

Two weeks later, strain off all solids and bottle your cologne in a dark bottle.

Lady of the Lake Oil

1/4 ounce almond oil,

15 drops orange oil

 5 drops rose oil,

1 drop cinnamon oil,

4 drops thyme oil,

14 drops chamomile oil,

2 drops ginger oil

combine all oils and shake vigorously. Store in an airtight, amber or dark bottle. Use on pulse points as a perfume or cologne.

Star Oil

1/4 ounce grapeseed oil

10 drops lemon oil

7 drops jasmine oil

7 drops rosemary oil

17 drops chamomile oil

4 drops sage oil

Combine all oils and shake vigorously. Store in an airtight, amber or dark bottle. Use on pulse points as a perfume or cologne.

Full Moon Oil I

13 drops of sandalwood essential oil

9 drops of vanilla essential oil or extract

3 drops of mango essential oil

1 drop amber essential oil

Mix prior to a full moon.

Charge in a clear container in the light of the full moon.

Use to anoint candles or yourself for full moon rituals.

Remember to move the potion to an amber bottle for storage.

Protection Potion

2-4 Cups of Spring Water, as a base

1 Tble. Powdered Iron or Iron Shavings

1 tsp. Vervain

1 tbsp sage oil

1 pinch hair of a coyote, fox, or wolf

This potion is not to be taken internally! Use it to consecrate an object or space.

Sleep Spell and Oil

1/2 oz grapeseed or apricot kernal oil

12 drops chamomile oil

3 drops lavender

3 drops eucalyptus oil

Mix the oils and use as a perfume just before going to sleep.

Love and Admiration Oil

10 drops patchouli
2 drops jasmine
1 drop of ylang ylang

Mix the oils and leave the bottle where the full moonlight can strike it for three nights. Do not let the sunlight touch it. Bring it inside before the sun rises.

When you remove the bottle, replace it with

1 rose petal
1 piece rose quartz
5 almonds

Leave them in a place where the Sun can see them, making sure to move them before moonlight can strike them. On the fourth day, mix together the two sets of ingredients and leave in a dark place. Wear the oils and rose quartz etc is a sachet. Carry it in your purse or pocket when you wish to draw love and admiration to yourself.

Lust Potion

6 drops of Sandalwood oil

6 drops of Rose oil

6 drops of Clove oil

6 drops of Nutmeg oil

Wear as a perfume whenever you'll be in the presence of the person you're trying to attract.

Attraction Oil

7 drops rose oil

7 drops orange oil

1 clove

7 drops vanilla

Wear as a perfume and store in an airtight amber bottle.

Aphrodite Oil

3 drops Jasmine

3 drops Rose

1 drop Lavender

2 drops Vanilla

1 drop Patchouli

1 drop Beragmot

On a Friday night blend the oils. This oil should only be worn by women wishing to attract men.

Protection Oil

1 tbsp grapeseed oil

4 drops cinnamon oil

4 drops vanilla oil

2 drops sandalwood oil

Use the oil on yourself or to consecrate items or a space.

Prosperity Potion

One part sandalwood oil
One part sage oil
One part clove bud oil
One part amber oil
One part nutmeg oil

Rub the oil on a piece of jade to carry in a sachet or pocket for extra strong effect.

Seawoman Oil

1 pinch Seaweed or one strip of dried seaweed
1 Seashell
A pinch of Sea Salt
1 cup sea water

mix ingredients and use to anoint candles, talismans, amulets, or other objects.

General Anointment Oil

1 handful mint or spearmint leaves

1 handful thyme

1 pinch ginger

1 oz grapeseed or apricot kernel oil

4 oz beeswax

melt the beeswax in a double boiler and add the leaves and oil. Strain the leaves out eventually if you wish but it might be nice to have chunks of leaves and herbs in the ointment. Cool and use to anoint sacred objects, or yourself.

Full Moon Oil II

13 drops of sandalwood essential oil

9 drops of vanilla essential oil or extract

3 drops jasmine oil

3 drops of jasmine essential oil

1 drop of rose essential oil

Mix prior to a full moon. Charge in a clear container or vial in the light of the full moon. Use to anoint candles or yourself for full moon rituals or just when you want to feel some of the moon's energy.

Truth Oil

3 drops Sage

3 drops Lavender

2 drops Pine

1 pinch marigold leaves

1 pinch nutmeg

Blend together and use to anoint objects, or yourself. It will inspire others around you to tell the truth.

Banishing Oil

½ oz apricot kernel oil

7 drops pepper oil or pinch of pepper (cayenne works best)

10 drops peppermint oil

12 drops of rue or rosemary oil.

1 handful pine needles

1 bundle dried sage

1 black onyx stone

Simply mix the ingredients, and strain out the herbs after a week. Do not anoint yourself with this oil as it is very strong. Use it to sprinkle on a space or surface. As you do it, focus on the person or energies you wish to banish.

Third Eye Oil

1 part amber oil
1 part vanilla oil
½ part cinnamon oil

Use this on your third eye. To make it more potent, store a small amethyst in the bottle along with it. Be careful, however, because it is potent and will irritate the mucous membranes.

Holyday Oil

1 part frankincense
1 part myrrh
1 part sage
½ part cinnamon
½ part lemon peel
¼ part ginger

Mix, and use for anointing.

Spray with Oils

1/4 cup high quality vodka

¼ cup rose water

3 tbsp almond oil

Pour all ingredients into a spray pump bottle and close.
Shake the bottle until well mixed. Shake before each use.

EARTH MAGICK: IN THE GARDEN

Cultivating and growing your own garden is one of the best ways to enjoy and bask in the earth's energy. It will allow you to mix your own brews, potions, and tinctures with that much more of your own energy. You can rest assured that your herbs were not poisoned with harsh chemicals, or cultivated by workers in poor conditions. Even if you have no outdoor space in which to make a garden, you can have a collection of potted plants that will more than suffice.

Planting a Garden

The planting of a new herb garden should ideally take place in the spring or summer in northern climates, but they can usually be planted year-round in more temperate climates.

Before planting you will want to prepare the land, physically and ritually. Choose the plot of land, and clear the weeds from it. Return at night, preferably on a waxing moon, and cast a circle around the boundary of your herb garden. Set a candle at the four compass points. This done, draw a five-pointed star in the circle. You can draw it with your finger, by carving a line in the soil, or you can sprinkle powdered mistletoe or sage to draw the lines. Once this is done, go to each point and ask the powers of the North,

South, East and West to protect the garden. Sit in meditation for awhile, then put out the candles starting with the North. The next morning, pour a glass of apple cider vinegar into the ground, and then say a prayer to thank the God and Goddess for their blessings.

As you plant your seedlings or bulbs, have in mind the magical/ritual purposes for the herb. You will want to plant according to the phases of the moon. If the useful part of the plant is the leaf, stem, or flower, then plant it during the waxing moon. Trees and root herbs should be planted during the waning moon. Talk to your plants, and meditate on them, giving them positive energy.

Once your herbs have grown, you should make an effort to gather what you will need for that day in the morning, before the strong sunlight can evaporate the essential oils.

There are traditions to follow all year long in the garden. On the Autumn Equinox, go out to the garden and find some herbs with seeds ready for gathering. Pick some of them, visualizing the new, unborn life within them. At Yule, place candles on a Yule log. Then the next morning, return with the candle drippings or ash from the yule log. Sprinkle them in your garden, or bury them while thanking the goddess and the god. On the Spring Equinox you will want to bless the seeds that you gathered of the Autumn Equinox.

Potting Soil

1 part finished compost

1 part loose garden or commercial potting soil

Peet Moss Soil

1 part commercial potting soil or leaf mold

1 part sphagnum or peat moss

1 part perlite

Limestone potting soil

4 parts loose garden potting soil

2 parts peat moss

2 parts compost

2 parts vermiculite

6 teaspoons dolomitic limestone (the limestone helps to neutralize the acids in the leaf mold and peat moss)

IV. EARTH MAGICK WITH CRYSTALS

Crystals are a powerful repository of the Earth's energy. Herbs, of course, have an incredible ability to heal the physical body via topical and internal application, and can even uplift the spirit when used for aroma therapeutic purposes in perfumes and oils. Crystals, however, can be a very useful tool to have for treating ailments of the spirit, and to give energy to your magickal workings.

BASIC CRYSTAL SELECTION AND CARE

Crystals can be chosen to aid in specific spells, and for meditative practices. When it comes to selecting the crystals you will work with, I would recommend that you go to a store that will allow you to not only look at, but touch them. You will find that the right crystal will identify itself quickly. Though there are many reputable online stores that sell crystals, it is difficult to asses their individual energies and vibrations without touching and holding them.

While perusing gems and crystals you may find that a particular item draws you to it. Follow your instincts. Your body and psyche needs all 7 colors: red, orange, yellow, green, blue, indigo and violet and you may unconsciously be drawn to the gems or crystals that are most appropriate for you.

CHARGING & CLEASING OF CRYSTALS

Before you start to use your crystals you should clean and charge them to remove any negative energy or vibrations from others who may have handled them. There are several easy ways to cleanse your crystals:

Bathing

Soak your crystal in one cup of sea salt dissolved in one quart of purified or spring water. Use a glass or porcelain bowl as silver or copper may interfere with the crystals' natural vibrations. When you place them in the bowl, meditate on them and ask that they are cleared. Leave them for at least an hour but they can soak for a day without harm.

Sunshine Bath

Place your crystal in direct sunlight for at least four hours.
When you place each crystal, meditate and ask that the
crystal is cleared.

Moonlight Bath

Place your crystal in the light of a full moon for at least four
ours. When you place each crystal, meditate and ask that
the crystal is cleared.

Burying

Wrap your crystal in cotton, silk or linen and bury it in a
place you feel comfortable for at least 24 hours.

After you have used one or more of these methods, they are
ready to be charged. You will learn about charging
Magickal objects in the section about your wand. The
lesson in that section can be applied to any talisman or
Magickal object. After cleansing and charging you should
never let anyone touch your crystals. Should this

accidentally happen, clean and charge them again before using them in your work

PROPERTIES OF CRYSTALS, STONES, AND GEMS

AVENTURINE: A good luck stone, especially in financial matters. Stimulates creativity, intelligence and perception. A great healing stone, it clears negative energy and vibrations as well as restoring general well being.

AGATE: General protection and healing, increases courage, self-confidence, and energy and promotes longevity. Solid, grounding.

AMETHYST: Reduces negative emotions (anger, impatience, nightmares); improves psychic abilities and imagery.

BLOODSTONE: An intense healing stone. It revitalizes love, relationships and friendships. It brings purification, orderliness, prosperity, and instills wisdom, enhances creativity, and supports decision making. Warrior stone for overcoming obstacles, calm ones fears of a real or perceived enemy, Boosts strength and courage and attracts wealth, healing, charity.

CITRINE: Reduces anxiety, fear, and depression; improves problem-solving, memory, willpower, and clarity.

CLEAR QUARTZ: Inner strength, amplifies the properties of other gemstones, strength. Probably the most versatile multi-purpose healing stone. Easy to cleanse, store info/energy in, program or amplify energy and healing with. Can both draw and send energy. Powerful clear ones for meditation, sending & receiving guidance. Stimulates natural crystals in body tissue and fluids to resonate at new healing frequency. The greatest of all healing stones. Acts as an amplifier for psychic energy and aids meditation and visualization.

CARNELIAN: Improves physical energy, confidence, assertiveness; stimulate appetite, emotions, sexuality.

FLUORITE: Assists the conscious mind and body in analyzing conditions and situations in a rational and non-emotional manner, it enables detachment of the mind from the emotions so that the thought process can utilize the intuitive in achieving a higher level of self understanding. Mental clarity. Helps to tap creative resources and experience the inner self. Enhances spiritual energy work, focuses the will and balances the psyche. Enhances ability to concentrate.

GOLDSTONE: Uplifting, reduces tension and stomach problems.

HEMATITE: One of the most grounding of all stones. Condenses confusion into mental clarity, concentration, memory, practicality, helps study, bookkeeping, detail work, sound sleep. Confidence, will power, boldness. Egyptians used it to calm hysteria and anxiety. Helps adjust to being physical. Enables the psychic practitioner to unfocus from the physical world so as to receive psychic information. Aids in developing the psychic mental mind, optimism, grounds ideas, anti-depression. Calms and soothes, eases stress. Great stone for grounding.

JADE: Emotional balance, humility, harmony, wealth, longevity, compassion.

JASPER: (Yellow, orange, brown, green) Jasper is known as the "supreme nurturer" It reminds us that we are not here on this physical plane just for ourselves but also here to bring joy and substance to others, assisting others in releasing the bonds of negative energy. It is the stone that protects against negativity and helps one to be grounded to the stabilizing energy of the earth. Use this stone for long periods of hospitalization and when your energy feels low.

JASPER: (red) Powerful stone used for divination practice, worn to protect the individual during out of body experiences and vision quests by providing a solid grounding. It helps with conflict and aggression. Promotes grace and perseverance.

LAPIS LAZULI: Reduces anxiety, restlessness, insomnia, and shyness.

MALACHITE: Reduces depression & anger. Stimulates vision & concentration.

MOONSTONE: Soothes stress, anxiety, Enhances intuitive sensitivity via feelings and less overwhelmed by personal feelings. Greater flexibility and flow of life. For emotional balance, gracefulness. Balance of Ying-Yang energy. Can open your heart to love. It is also helpful in psychic work. It opens the spirit to the feminine aspect.

MOSS AGATE: Promotes agreeability, persuasiveness and strength in all endeavors. Improves self-esteem. Moss agate was used by the Native Americans as a power stone for the art of "cloud-busting" to bring rain. It is also said to help one in the acquisition of riches.

MOTHER OF PEARL: Wealth

ONYX: Protection. This stone helps to change bad habits, it is also an excellent grounding stone. Absorbs and flattens emotional intensity. Used for self-protection and to keep away bothersome relationships. Helps to release old relationships and keep away general negativity.

RHODONITE: Promotes self-esteem, self-worth and self-confidence, self-affirmation and self-love. Fosters ability to remain calm in arguments and resolve disagreements in a loving way.

ROSE QUARTZ: Emotional balance, love, beauty, peacefulness, kindness & self-esteem.

SAPPHIRE QUARTZ: A good healing stone to expand self expression and creativity, plus refining communication skills to new levels.

SNOWFLAKE OBSIDIAN: For grounding the physical and for protection. Used as a scrying tool to help the psychic unfocus from the physical and venture inward to receive information. Legendary dispeller of negativity, protects against nightmares and emotional draining.

SOLADITE: Healing of emotions and physical body. Assures clear communication. Eliminates guilt and fears and brings about clear vision. Elicits deep thought and calms overreaction by enabling one to think clearly.

TIGERSEYE: For protection, divination and inquiry into past or future lives. Clarity, optimism, and creativity. Enhances psychic ability. Stimulates wealth and helps to maintain it.

TOPAZ: The most powerful, electromagnetic of yellow/solar plexus gems. A strong, steady, high level gem for mental clarity, focus, perceptively, high level concepts, confidence, personal power, stamina. Helps with mood swings, insomnia, worries, fears, depression, exhaustion, nervous system stress, stomach anxiety. Radiates warmth, sun/light energy, protection. Brings emotions and thinking into balance. One can focus their desires through this stone, visual images in the mind are transformed into universal messages. Enables communication from other realms in the universe. Promotes peace and calms emotions, as well as promoting forgiveness.

TURQUOISE: A master healing stone that promotes spontaneity in romance and stimulates the initiation of romantic love. It balances and aligns all charkas and subtle bodies and can bring all energies to a higher level. A highly spiritual stone, yet grounding, it brings soothing energy and peace of mind. It brings strength, wisdom, protection, and positive thinking. A good general healer for all illnesses and excellent conductor. This gentle, cool, soothing stone is a Native American classic. For open communication, creativity, serenity, spiritual bonding, and upliftment. It opens the heart for giving/receiving. It symbolizes our source (spirit/sky) and spiritual love for healing, and help. Turquoise is the ancient absorber of "negativity".

UNIKITE: Healing of the soul. Guide to transformation and higher self. Reconciliation. Promotes balance and emotional stability. Transforms negative emotions into positive ones. A grounding stone.

CRYSTALS FOR SPECIFIC RESULTS

READINESS FOR ACTION: Amethyst, Ametrine, Fire Opal, Chrysoprase, Rhodonite, Turquoise

NEW BEGINNINGS: Garnet

CHEERFULNESS: Amber, Fire Opal

CREATIVITY: Ametrine, Amber, Garnet, Labradorite, Tourmaline

UNFINISHED BUSINESS: Aquamarine, Carnelian

FULFILLMENT OF DESIRES: Amber, Malachite, Hematite, Fire Opal

DEVOTION: Kunzite, Tourmaline

SOLVING DIFFICULTIES: Carnelian, Garnet, Moss Agate, Smokey Quartz, Tiger Eye

CONNECTION WITH EARTH: Petrified Wood

ENTHUSIASM: Aventurine, Fire Opal, Garnet, Labradorite, Rhodochrosite

FERTILITY: Chrysoprase, Imperial Toopaz, Moonstone, Rhodonite, Rose Quartz

FORESIGHT: Aquamarine, Turquoise

FRIENDSHIP: Emerald, Lapis Lazuli, Malachite, Peridot, Rhodonite, Watermelon Tourmaline

GOAL SETTING: Labradorite, Lepidolite, Watermelon Tourmaline

INDUSTRIOUSNESS: Rhodochrosite

INTUITION: Amethyst, Amazonite, Ametrine, Petrified Wood, Kunzite, Labradorite, Moonstone, Turquoise

LOVE: Chrysoprase, Emerald, Moonstone, Rhodochrosite, Rose Quartz, Ruby, Watermelon Tourmaline

LUCK: Agate, Ametrine, Aventurine, Amber, Chrysoprase, Garnet, Malachite, Moonstone, Sunstone, Turquoise

INCREASE MOTIVATION: Amber, Chrysoprase

ORDER: Aquamarine, Fluorite, Sodalite

POSITIVE ATTITUDE TOWARDS LIFE: Malachite, Chrysoprase, Imperial Topaz, Rhodochrosite, Sunstone

PROTECTION: Agate, Lepidolite, Smokey Quartz, Serpentine, Tiger Eye, Turquoise, Black Tourmaline, Watermelon Tourmaline

SELF-CONFIDENCE: Calcite, Citrine, Fluorite, Garnet, Imperial Topaz, Sunstone

STAMINS: Aquamarine, Garnet, Red Jasper

LOGICAL THINKING: Agate, Chrysoprase, Citrine, Kunzite, Lepidolite, Black Tourmaline

V. WORKING WITH THE ELEMENTS: WATER MAGICK

Water Energy

Direction: West

Color: Blue

Elemental: Undines

Time of Day: Twilight

Season: Autumn

Tools: Cauldron and chalice

Zodiac: Cancer, Pisces, Scorpio

Animals: Dolphins, fish, whales, all creatures of the sea, serpents

Places: Oceans, rivers, lakes, marshes, pools, swamps, bogs, streams, rainforests, etc.

BASICS OF BREWMASTERY

A "brew", as used in this book, indicates an infusion, decoction, potion, or tea. Most of the herbs listed in the previous section can be ingested, but there are a couple exceptions. BEFORE YOU INGEST ANY HERB, MAKE SURE IT IS NOT POISONOUS! You can do this over the web, of course, or with any reputable herbal medicine dictionary or encyclopedia.

That said, brews are a wonderfully inexpensive and natural way to cure ailments of the body, mind, and spirit. Brews also represent a marriage between water and earth energy.

ENERGY FROM THE WATER

The type of water used when making a brew to be ingested is important. Well, spring, filtered, and distilled waters are preferred, but be wary of bottled waters. Not all bottled waters are created equal. Aquafina and Dasani, for example, are merely bottled tap water. Aquafina, if I remember correctly, is the tap water of Riverside County, but bottled.

Tap water, in many areas, far surpasses the quality of 2/3rds of the bottled waters out there. No joke—there are no federal regulations, and few state regulations, on bottled water, and plenty of regulations on tap water. Have you ever heard of any American dying from consuming tap water? Never, right? Despite the bad rap that tap water gets, it's among the safest water in the world.

Also, bottled water creates ridiculous amounts of non-biodegradable waste. Every piece of plastic ever produced still exists in some landfill somewhere. And another important point to remember is that plastic comes from oil. Don't get me started on the dangers of oil dependency, both foreign and domestic. So to make a long story short: getting a Britta filter and filtering your tap water will give you water that is just as good as most bottled waters out there, and will cause less waste and less pollution.

HEATING THE BREW

Putting a kettle on a stove or over a fire is your best bet. I guess you could prepare a brew in a microwave oven, but this isn't the best idea. It could be in my head, but somehow, I feel like foods and liquids heated in a microwave just don't taste as good.

TOOLS AND VESSELS

You don't need much to make a good brew: you'll just want a good quality tea kettle, a tea pot, and a clear jar for solar or lunar teas. Some prefer to dry and prepare the herbs themselves, in which case you may find a mortar and pestle handy. You'll probably want to consecrate and purify each of your tools before you use them.

WATER RECIPES

Aphrodite Lust Drink

2 tsp. Black Tea

1 pinch Coriander

3 fresh Mint leaves (or 1/2 tsp. dried)

5 fresh Rosebud petals (or 1 tsp. dried)

½ tsp dried lemon peel

1 pinche Nutmeg

3 pieces Orange peel

Place all ingredients into teapot. Boil three cups or so of water and add to the pot. Sweeten with honey or maple syrup.

Venus Lust Drink

5 parts Rose petals

1/2 part Clove

1/2 part Nutmeg

1 part ginger

1 tsp honey (to taste)

Make as a normal tea.

Chakra Opening Brew

3 parts Rose petals

1 part Cinnamon

1/2 part Nutmeg

½ part clove

½ part black tea

Place in teapot, fill with boiling water, let steep, covered, for a few minutes. Let it steep and then drink with honey, if desired.

Sweet Dreams Tea

1 part chamomile

1 part lavender

½ part spearmint (not peppermint)

Mix and let steep until cool enough to drink. Then drink before bed.

Headache Brew

1 pinch White Willow bark

1 pinch peppermint

1 lemon wedge

Brew and drink a half a cup as needed. Can be used daily. DO NOT TAKE IF YOU ARE PREGNANT OR LACTATING.

Sleep Brew

1 part chamomile
1 part lavender
1 part valerian

Drink one cup before bed.

almost all grocery stores.

Rosemary Tea

Useful for: general aches and pains, lack of energy

Directions: boil water, and add one teaspoon of crushed or dried rosemary. Pour through a strainer and serve. Honey may be used as a sweetener

Ginger Tea

Useful for: asthma, respiratory problems

Directions: add ¼ teaspoon of ginger to ½ cup of hot water. Take two tablespoons before bedtime.

Holy Basil Tea

Useful for: chronic bronchitis; chronic irritation of the upper respiratory tract

1 tablespoon of basil

2cups of hot water.

Directions: Take two tablespoons four times per day

Cinnamon Tea
Useful for: congestion; common cold

3 g. bark

1 ½ cups of hot water.

Directions: Steep and drink at bedtime as tea.

Cayenne Pepper Shot

Useful for: extreme congestion, sinus infection

1 c. hot water.

1 tsp lemon juice

1 garlic clove put through a garlic press

1 pinch cayenne pepper.

Directions: Mix well and take as a shot.

Fennel Linseed Tea

Useful for: constipation

1/3 tea spoon Fennel seeds, powdered
1/3 tea spoon Linseed seeds, powdered
1/3 tea spoon Liquorice root, powdered
1 3/4 cups Water

Combine equal quantities of the three herbs and add this herb mixture to the water and boil, covered, for 10 minutes. Filter the tea before drinking.

Dosage: 1 cup, 3 times a day.

Black Pepper Tea

Useful for: diarrhea

5 crushed pepper seeds

1 c. water

Directions: Boil the seeds in the water for 15 minutes in a covered container. Remove from the heat and strain. Take 1⁄2 tea spoon, twice a day.

Ginger Mint Tea

Useful for: fever

2g crushed ginger

2g crushed mint leaves

1 ½ c. hot water

Directions: Mix the 2 herbs in the water and bring to a boil. Cover and cook for 15 minutes. Strain the decoction and drink.

Lemon Tea

Useful for: cold, fever

1 lemon slice
1 cup hot water

Directions: bring water to a boil. Pour a cup and add the lemon slice. Sip slowly.

Yarrow Tea

Useful for: piles

1-2 tea spoon Herb/blossoms, crushed
1 cup Water

Directions: prepare the infusion by combining the herb with the water in a covered container. Let the mixture stand for 5-6 hours. Strain before drinking.

Coriander Infusion

Useful for: impotence

Leaves, chopped 1 tea spoon
Boiling water 1 cup

To make the infusion, cover the leaves with boiling water, close the lid of the teapot and leave for 15 minutes, then strain.

Dosage: 2-4 table spoon a day.

Remember: coriander leaf extract acts as an aphrodisiac, while

Coriander seed extract suppresses the sex drive.

Mint Tea

Useful for: stomach pain

1 tea spoon spearmint leaves, crushed
2 cups Water

Combine the spearmint leaves and the water and raise the mixture to a boil in a covered container. Remove from the heat and let the tea stand for 15 minutes. Strain before drinking.

Dosage: 1-2 cups a day.

Ginger Infusion

Useful for: painful menstruation

6 g Embelia, whole plant, powdered
6 g Ginger, dried, powdered
1 3/4 cups Water
6 g Sugar

Mix the two herbs and boil. Remove from the heat, strain and sweeten with the sugar.

Dosage: 3/4 cup a day.

Onion Cold Relief

Useful for: extreme congestion; chest colds

1 onion, sliced

Merely keep the sliced onion by the bed of a person who is suffering from horrific chest congestion. A personal testimonial: I once was so sick that I couldn't sleep unless I was sitting up. Otherwise I would be overcome with wracking coughs. I tried everything: codeine, robitussin, liquor, lemon juice, a cayenne pepper shot, a chest rub...nothing worked. I could not sleep. Finally I received a suggestion to slice an onion and leave it by my bed. My room smelled for three days, but I was finally able to sleep peacefully.

Natural Flu Relief

Useful for: relief from the flu

2 teaspoons cayenne pepper
1 ½ teaspoons salt
1 cup hot chamomile tea
1 cup apple cider vinegar
juice from 1 lemon slice

Make chamomile tea. While it is steeping, grind the cayenne pepper and salt together. Add the hot chamomile tea, let it cool, and then add the vinegar. Take a tablespoon or so every half hour.

VI. BATH MAGICK WITH OILS & HERBS

The bath can be an excellent place to put together your knowledge of herbs and oils. Ritual baths are, of course, necessary to prepare for many spells and Magickal workings. They can also be a great way to relax, or be Magickal workings in and of themselves. Before using any herbs or oils in the bath, however, make sure that you're not allergic to them! Bathwater can creep into some pretty sensitive areas, and the last thing you want is to irritate sensitive parts of the skin!

Protection Bath

You will need:

1 tsp basil
1 cup boiling spring water

Steep a teaspoon of basil in a cup of boiling water, and strain out the herb. Add it to the bathwater, and enjoy!

Lavender Bath

You will need:

Lavender colored candle
1 tsp lavender flowers
1 tsp chamomile flowers
1 tsp rosemary
1 tbsp lemon juice
1 square foot of muslin or cheesecloth
lavender ribbon

To begin, cast a circle in your bathroom. Call the elements, and light the candle. Then blend the herbs, and put them in the fabric. Tie the fabric using a ribbon so that you have made a little sachet. Put it in the bathwater, and then add the lemon juice.

When you settle into the tub, lean back, relax, and take three deep breaths. Meditate and relax.

Lavender Bath Salts

1⁄2 cup sea salt

1⁄4 cup Epsom salts

1⁄4 cup dead sea mineral salts

40 drops lavender essential oil

Mix all ingredients well, then add the essential oil. Use one half cup for your bath. To begin, cast a circle. Then add the bath salt as the water fills the tub.

When you enter the tub, center yourself, and meditate.

Healing Bath

You will need:

¼ cup dead sea salts
1 tsp dried lavender
5 drops lavender oil.
Muslin sachet

Fill your muslin bag half way with the dead sea salts, add two teaspoons of lavender herb
and one drop of lavender oil. Tie up the bag and include in your bath. As you slide in to the tub, relax and visualize any aches, pains, or negative energy being lifted from you, and away.

Bath Bomb

You will need:

4 cups Epsom salts
2 cups Sea salt
1 cup non fat powdered milk
2 cups oatmeal ground to a very fine powder in blender or
food processor.
40 drops of essential oil

Bath bombs are delightfully fizzy, and make any bath a
pleasure. If you wish to relax in the bath, I'd advocate
choosing lavender, violet, or chamomile essential oil. Mix
everything together, put it through a sieve, and then add
the oil. Add it slowly--10 drops at a time, and mix it. Add it
to your bath and enjoy!

Sinus Relief Bath

You will need

1/2 cup each of dried yarrow flowers

½ dried mint leaves

½ cup dried rose petals.

½ cup comfrey leaves

1 tbsp lemon juice

Place the herbs in muslin, cheesecloth or nylon. Tie it off and and let it steep in the bath for a few minutes, like a giant tea bag. You can use the bundle to exfoliate as well.

Cleansing and Purifying Bath

You will need

½ cup dried rose petals.

1 tbls bicarbonate soda

5 drops essential oil

1 tsp. almond or apricot kernel oil

½ cup sea salt

Stir the soda, essential oil, lemon juice and oil together and then blend in the salt.

Dissolve in the bath water. Call the elements, cast a circle, and place candles at the 4 corners of the tub.

Step slowly into the bath water, feeling it envelope around you. Close your eyes. Say, aloud or to yourself:

All is well, all is blessed

Time in here is time for rest

Fly away on swift wings

Aches, pains, evil things.

Mental Rejuvenation Bath

You will need

10 drops almond oil

10 drops cypress oil,

10 drops lavender oil.

4 blue candles

Anoint your hand with sandalwood oil and skim your hand over the surface of the water four times.

Then enter the bath and meditate away any sources of mental or physical stress.

Bath for Muscle Aches

You will need:

2 tsp dried thyme (This herb is a great muscle relaxant.)

2 tsp dried rosemary

2 tsp lavender

2 tsp Epsom salt

bath sachet or muslin, cheesecloth, or nylon bag.

Mix the herbs and place in the cloth or bath sachet. Soak as long as you need so as to do away with muscle aches and pains

VII. WORKING WITH THE ELEMENTS: FIRE MAGICK

Fire Energy

Direction: South

Colors: Red and orange

Elemental: Salamander

Time of Day: Noon

Season: Summer

Tools: Wand, candle, and staf

Zodiac: Aries, Leo, Sagittarius

Animals: Dragons, snakes, lizards, and phoenixes

Places: Deserts, volcanoes, Earth's core

Fire energy is the power of the most intense emotion, such as anger, lust, and love. Just like the element itself, fire energy is difficult to control and, if left unchecked, can destroy everything in its path. When contained, the energy can provide "light", revealing the truth to its holder. A contained flame, like in a candle or in hot coals, is much more valuable. It is more than enough for magic, but not enough to overpower the worker of the magick

.

CANDLE MAGICK

Candle magick is a very powerful form of fire magick. Candles are a part of most spells and incantations, and understanding how to properly use candles is an important part of Wicca.

Flame is, obviously, fire energy. When you use a candle, your work will be infused with fire energy. Selecting the appropriate color candle will help you focus the nature of the energy.

CANDLE COLORS WITH A PURPOSE:

White

* The Goddess
* Higher Self
* Purity
* Peace
* Cleanliness

Black

* Binding
* Shapeshifting
* Protection
* Shields from negative spirits

Brown

* friendship

Silver

* goddess energy
* Astral energy
* Female energy
* Night energy
* Intuition
* Dreams

Purple

* Third Eye
* Psychic Ability
* Hidden Knowledge
* Spiritual Power

Natural Elements and the Witch

Blue

* Water energy
* Protection
* Calm
* Good Fortune
* Communication
* Spiritual Inspiration

Green

* Earth energy
* Physical Healing
* Prosperity
* Tree and Plant Magic
* Growth

Pink

* Romantic love
* Romance
* Affection
* Nurturing

Red

* magnifies fire energy
* Passion
* Strength
* decisiveness
* Lust
* Aggression
* Survival
* Sexual energy
* Masculine energy

Orange

* Spiritual Success
* Property Deals
* Friendship
* Justice

Gold

* God energy
* Promote Winning
* Male energy
* Happiness
* Exuberance
* Sun energy

Yellow

* The Element of Air
* Intelligence
* Logic

It is also possible to manipulate the color of the flame using the following chemicals:

Green flame: Borax or Boric acid, copper nitrates or barium nitrates

Orange flame: calcium chloride

Red flame: stronium nitrate

Yellow flame: Sodium Chorate or Potassium Nitrate

Purple flame: Lithium Chlorate

To change the flame of a Fire: Put three level spoons of the chemical into a paper cup; fill 1/2 full with water and stir. Soak several small chips of wood in this solution overnight. The next day, remove the chips with tweezers and lay on newspaper to dry. They can now be added to your fireplace to produce bright colors.

To change the flame of the candle: when you make the candle, the wicks will have to be soaked in the chemical. Three level spoons of the chemical should be mixed in ½ water, and the wicks should soak in it and then dry. Be careful if you have sensitive skin!

CANDLE SPELLS

One of the simplest of magical arts which comes under the heading of natural magic is candle burning. The materials are easy to obtain and use an object with which we are all familiar—a candle.

The size and shape of the candles you use is unimportant, although decorative, extra large, ornate, scented, or unusually shaped candles will not be suitable as these may create distractions. The simple slender candles sold for use in the home is perfectly fine, if not ideal. Those who are feeling particularly industrious can make his or her own. Candle kits can be found at specialty and craft stores, and are easy to use.

The candles you use for any type of magical use should be completely unused, and no one but yourself should touch it. Under no circumstances use a candle which has already been lit, even for the most benign purpose. Vibrations picked up by secondhand materials or equipment may disturb and pollute your work.

Once you have purchased or made your ritual candle it has to be 'dressed' before burning so as to establish a psychic link between it and you. By touching the candle during the dressing procedure, you are charging it with our own personal energy and also concentrating the desire of your magical act into the wax. The candle, in this sense, almost becomes like a wand, and is an extension of you. Make sure you dress the candle before it is lit.

To dress it, point the candle to the north. Use a compass to make sure that you are pointing it in the right direction. Rub oil into the candle beginning at the top or North end and work downwards to the half-way point. Always brush in the same direction downwards. This process is then repeated by beginning at the bottom or south end and working up to the middle. The oil that you use is important. This will be discussed later in detail.

The candles you use can be colored in accordance with the following magical uses:

White- peace and innocence.

Red- strength, courage, sexual potency.

Pink- love and romance.

Yellow- memory

Green- fertility and luck

Blue-protection from evil

Purple- luck in finances

Orange—career matters

For instance, if you wanted to use candle magic to enrich your sex life, you would select a red candle to burn. To pass an exam, burn a yellow candle.

The simplest form of candle magic is to write down your goal on a clean, unused piece of paper. Use paper in a color that matches the candle. As you write your goal, visualize your dream coming true. Visualize your boss giving you a raise, or your business selling out of its product because it has become a wild success.

After you have written down your goal and meditated on it, carefully fold the paper four times. Place the end of the folded paper in the candle flame and set light to it. As it burns, focus on your goal.

Allow the candle to burn till it goes out. Take normal fire safety precautions and keep watch over it as it burns.

If you are conducting a magical ritual which involves another person, such as sending healing powers to a sick person, the second person can be symbolically present during the ritual by another candle.

IMPORTANT ASPECTS OF CANDLE MAGICK

In dealing with Candle Magick, it is first and foremost best to learn about. Despite the fact that working with candles is regarded as Fire magick, the candle itself contains the element of water, air and earth. When lit, the elements of fire and the spirit are added to these elements.

☐The shape of the burned wax when left to flow on its own can also be very revealing, and you can use the shape of the candle and its drippings for divination. ☐Remember that each candle is different as our own personal wish.

☐The flame or halo of the candle is the life of the fire itself. Upon lighting the wick, we have now included the elements of Fire and Spirit, guided by human hands and by your spell or magickal working.

CANDLE MAKING

Candle making is not terribly difficult. It is a wonderful activity to plan for your family, or your coven. You can make the candles the color you want, and with the oils that you want. You can also infuse the candles with your energy, which benefits your magickal workings.

You will need:

Coffee can
Pot
Wax paper or foil
Crayon or candle dye
Wick (from crafts store)
Fire extinguisher (for safety)
Wooden spoon
Paraffin wax or old stumps of old candles
Heat proof containers
Cooking spray
Tooth picks
Wick Tabs (also from arts and crafts store)
Oils, herbs, stones (if desired.)

Place wax inside coffee, can and place the coffee can inside the pot. Fill a pot with water until you reach half way up the outside of the can. Heat it on low heat until the wax melts. When it melts, stir in crayons or coloring until it's the color you want.

When it's melted, smooth, and the color you want, take it off the heat. □Spray cooking spray inside your containers—you can use shot glasses, pyrex dishes, or even a coffee can as a mold. □Cut off a length of wick and attach it at the bottom of your container with a wick tab. □Wrap the top of the wick around a toothpick or stick and support it on top of the container. This way, the wick will be straight. □Now is the time to add your herbs, stones, or oils if you desire. □ Pour the melted wax into the container, using a funnel if you want.

After you have poured as many candles as you want, let them sit for 4-6 hours before attempting to remove them from the containers. You can even freeze them if you want. After removing the candles from the containers, wipe away the oily substance and let them sit for at least another 3-4 hours to dry.

To make tapered candles, melt the wax in the coffee can and add the coloring, just as you would do for a candle made in the mold. This time, however, when you remove the wax from the heat, dip the wick in the wax over and over and over and over and over again. Let it hang until it cools.

SAMPLE CANDLE SPELLS

Spell to Mend a Wounded Heart

To Ease a Broken Heart you will need the following ingredients (be sure to charge them all before you begin):

Strawberry tea (at least one teabag's worth)

Small wand or stick from a willow tree

Three drops of lavender oil.

pink candles (2)

a mirror

one pink drawstring bag

one quartz crystal

one bowl of china, crystal, or silver

one silver spoon

1 teaspoon dried jasmine

1 tsp. strawberry leaves

1 teaspoon cloves

20 drops strawberry oil

Arrange the materials on a small table. Light an unused, pink candle that has been rubbed in a drop of strawberry oil. Make sure that no one has touched the candle besides you, and make sure that the candle has never been used. Make strawberry tea and when the water is done boiling, let the tea steep. While it steeps, draw a bath and add the lavender. Do not use any light other than the pink candle's light to draw and take the bath.

When you rise from the bath, sip the strawberry tea. Put a dab of strawberry oil on your throat, wrists, and heart. Use the willow wand to cast two circles in a clockwise direction around the table that the materials rest on.

Rub two drops of strawberry oil on the second candle. Make sure that the wick end is pointed north as you do so. Light the second pink candle. Mix all remaining and oils and herbs—except for the strawberry tea leaves from the tea--in the bowl.

While you stir the mixture slowly clockwise with a silver spoon, look at yourself in the mirror and say aloud: "I see the Threefold Goddess within me. Then put the mixture in the pink bag with the crystal. You will carry it with you always. Every time you are tempted to dwell on that which wounded your heart, smell the bag full of herbs. Remind yourself that you are the Threefold Goddess, and you bask in the light of Diana.

When your heart is healed, bury the bag.

Home Protection Spell

You will need:

Small mirror
Seven white candles
Bundle of dried sage
Matches
Essential oil of your choosing.
Representation of the Goddess of your choosing.
Representation of the God of your choosing.

As always, the first step is to consecrate the space you will be using, take a ritual bath, and put on your ritual wear.

Place your God and Goddesses representations in the middle of the altar. The next step will be to dress your candles. Kneel before the altar. Using essential oil from an herb or tree with protective qualities, mentally visualize a wall of energy surrounding your home. Rub the candles with the oil, pointing the wicks North as you do so.

Next, go to your altar. After reaching a state of concentration, place a bundle of sage between the effigies of the Goddess and the God. Ring the sage and effigies with your candles. Turn to your Goddess effigy. Continuing to visualize the field of energy surrounding your home, say:

Lunar light protect me!

Then turn to the God and say:

Solar light protect me!

Repeat as you light each candle.

Now, holding the mirror, invoke the Goddess and say:

Great Goddess of the Light
Great Goddess of the Sea
Great Goddess of the Land
Let all darkness flee.

Standing before the altar, hold the mirror facing the candles so that it reflects their flames. Keeping the mirror toward the candles, move slowly clockwise around your altar seven times, repeating the invocation. Continue concentrating on the wall of energy that surrounds your home. Visualize the candle light burning away the bad energy in your home.

Then, invoke the God and say:

> *Great God of the Light*
> *Great God of the Sea*
> *Great God of the Land*
> *Let all darkness flee.*

As you say this, hold the mirror as you have been but move counter clockwise, repeating the invocations.

Charge your home with the protective light of the Goddess and God. Visualize the light streaming through your home and bathing it in light.

When finished, stand once again before the images. Thank the Goddess and the God in any words you wish. Put out the candles, tie them together with white cord and store them in a safe place.

Basic Prosperity Spell

This is a basic spell that if used correctly, will bring you money.

You will need:

1 gold candle
6 green candles
9 white candles
Pine oil
sea salt or, if you live near the ocean, sand.

Take your ritual bath, put on your ritual wear, and cast the circle. Then carefully dress all candles with pine oil.

Arrange the candles thusly on the altar:

Gold candle in the center
Green candles in a circle around gold candle
White candles in a circle around green candles.

To begin, sprinkle a circle of salt or sand around the altar. Start to concentrate. Visualize yourself walking down the street and finding money, a bank error in which you are given extra funds or even a mound of coupons to your oft-frequented stores.

Light the middle candle and envision the flame acting as a magnet for money.

Circle the altar three times clockwise, visualizing the luck you want.

Say the following three times:

> *As my heart be full with the Goddess' light*
> *Bring money into my sight.*

After the previous saying, snuff out the flames. Place the candles in a green bag, and put them away. Though they cannot be used for another spell, they can serve decorative purposes at a later date.

Natural Elements and the Witch

VIII. WORKING WITH THE ELEMENTS: AIR AND SKY MAGICK

Direction: East

Colors: Yellow and white

Elemental: Sprites or sylphs

Time of Day: Dawn

Season: Spring

Tools: Athame, sword, and censor

Zodiac: Aquarius, Gemini, Libra

Animals: Birds

Places: Windswept hills, mountain peaks, towers

Air energy is not as overpowering as other energies, though it is certainly plentiful. Air energy does not have as much physical power as earth or fire energy, but it has great advantages nonetheless. It is the energy of intellect, wisdom, and understanding. It also supports communication and friendship.

For Wiccans, the night sky is, in itself, magick. The heavenly bodies that glide through the sky can be sources of divination or magickal workings themselves.

ASTROLOGY

Astrology, in the most general sense, is a group of beliefs in which knowledge of the relative positions of celestial bodies can aid in divination and analysis.

Practitioners of astrology are referred to as Astrologists, and interpret the positions of certain celestial bodies' influence on the world and her human inhabitants.

Though the position of celestial body can be considered and evaluated in an Astrological reading, the Sun, Moon, the planets, and the stars are generally of the most importance. The frame of reference for determining their positions are the tropical or sidereal zodiacal signs, the horizon, and midheaven on the other. This latter frame is typically further divided into the twelve astrological houses, which correspond to the twelve signs of the zodiac.

Over the centuries, however, the twelve zodiacal signs in Western astrology have shifted to the point of no longer corresponding to the same part of the sky as their original constellations.

The zodiac is the belt or band of constellations through which the Sun, Moon, and planets move. Twelve cycles of the Moon — the months — coincide with one solar year, and as such, the designation of twelve zodiacal signs corresponding with twelve different constellations was a logical conclusion.

One's zodiacal sign is calculated to correspond to the moment of an individual's birth. The position of the sun in the sky gives the individual his or her sun sign; the position of the moon gives him or her a moon sign. Commonly, in the West, much attention has been given to the Sun signs. For example, in the horoscope section of a magazine, the signs listed are all sun signs. The moon sign, however, is just as important.

A complete horoscope goes far beyond merely the sun and the moon, however. A complete horoscope is a chart divided into twelve different celestial houses. On this chart appears the location of the various positions of heavenly bodies on a given date and time based on astronomical tables.

A horoscope charting the positions of the celestial bodies on the birthday of a subject will tell of the subject's personality, strengths, weaknesses, and future challenges. A horoscope of a particular day can have different meanings for people according to their respective astrological signs.

Astrology is far more complicated and elegant than most people realize. It goes above and beyond the mere act of flipping to the back of Glamour and reading a paragraph. Real astrology involves an intimate knowledge of astronomy, some physics, and a talent for divination. There are volumes of books on the market that can teach exactly how to make a chart, and how to interpret it for yourself or for another.

But basically, figuring out the position of one's moon, sun, and rising is enough for the beginner to start to notice the effect of the cosmos on his or her path and circumstance.

THE MOON

The moon can be regarded as the embodiment of the Goddess. Performing spells during the wrong phase of the moon can seriously weaken the spell, so it is important to be able to recognize the phases of the moon, and what this means for a magickal working.

When the moon is waxing, this means the moon is getting larger in the sky, moving from the New Moon towards the Full Moon. This is a time for spells that attract, that bring positive change, spells for love, good luck, growth. At this time the moon represents the Goddess in her Maiden aspect, and this period of the moon lasts approximately fourteen days.

Full Moon is when the moon has reached its fullest and forms a sphere in the sky. This is the best time for spells that transform or increase pyschic ability. It is also an excellent time for fertility spells and invocations to lunar goddesses. This is a time of strength, love and power. At this time the moon represents the Goddess in her Mother aspect, and lasts about three days.

Waning Moon means the moon is decreasing in size, moving from the Full Moon towards the New Moon. This is a time for spells that banish, release, or reverse. At this time the moon represents the Goddess in her Crone Aspect, and lasts approximately fourteen days.

As the moon circles the sky, she travels through the 12 astrological signs, just as the sun does. When the moon resides within the various signs, the sign influences the magickal aspect of the moon.

Spells focusing primarily on directing Earth energy should be preformed when the moon is in Taurus, Virgo, or Capricorn.. Spells using Air energy should be preformed when the moon is Gemini, Libra, Aquarius. Fire spells should be performed when the moon is in Aries, Leo, or Sagittarius. Water spells should be preformed when the moon is in: Cancer, Scorpio, Pisces.

Moon in ARIES is the best time for spells involving authority, rebirth, leadership; healing spells of the face and head.

Moon in TAURUS is the best time for spells involving love, money, acquisition; healing spells for the throat and neck.

Moon in GEMINI is the best time for spells involving communication, writing, travel; healing spells for the arms, hands, and lungs.

Moon in CANCER is the best time for spells involving the home and for honoring lunar gods and goddesses; healing of the chest and stomach.

Moon in LEO is the best time for spells involving authority, courage, fertility; healing of the upper back, spine, heart.

Moon in VIRGO is the best time for spells involving employment, health, diet; healing of the intestines and nervous system.

Moon in LIBRA is the best time for spells involving justice, unions, balance (spiritual and otherwise), artistry; healing of the lower back and kidneys.

Moon in SCORPIO is the best time for spells involving power, psychic growth, sex; healing of the reproductive organs.

Moon in SAGITTARIUS is the best time for spells involving travel, sports, truth, horses; healing of the liver and thighs.Moon in CAPRICORN is the best time for spells involving organization, ambition, career, politics; healing of the knees, bones, teeth, skin.

Moon in AQUARIUS is the best time for spells involving science, freedom, friendship, breaking bad habits or addictions; healing of the calves, ankles, blood.

Moon in PISCES is the best time for spells involving music, art, telepathy, dreams; healing of the feet and lymph glands.

In magick, timing is very important. There is a lot to keep track of, certainly! Not only the elements you are choosing to include in a spell, but what color candles you choose, what the moon is doing, and what phase she is in! Don't worry. This will eventually all become second nature to you.

SPELLWORK BY PURPOSE, REFERENCING LUNAR PHASE

Abundance: waxing to full moon.

Addictions (TO END): waning moon.

Artistic Creations: waxing to full moon.

Bad Habits (to break): waning moon.

Bad Luck (to reverse): waning moon.

Beauty and Health: full moon.

Bindings: waning moon.

Blessings: full moon.

Career Advancement: waxing moon.

Communication: full moon.

Curses, Hexes (to break): waning moon.

Divinations: waxing and full moons.

Energy Raising: waxing moon.

Exorcisms: waning moon.

Fear (overcoming): waning moon.

Fertility Rituals: waxing and full moons.

Forgiveness: new moon.

Friendship: waxing moon.

Garden Planting Spells: waxing moon.

Goals (attainment of): waxing to full moon.

Good Luck: waxing moon.

Growth (of an kind): waxing moon.

Harmony: waxing moon.

Happiness: waxing and full moons.

Healings (to increase health): waxing moon.

Healings (to end sickness): waning moon.

House Blessings: full moon.

Inspiration: waxing and full moons.

Intuition: full moon.

Jinx-Breaking: waning moon.

Judgment: waxing and full moons.

Liberation (to free oneself from something): waning moon.

Love Magick: waxing and full moons.

Love Spells (to reverse): waning moon.

Lunar Goddess Invocations: full moon.

Money Matters (to increase wealth): waxing moon.

Negativity (to banish): waning moon.

Nightmares (to banish): waning moon.

Obtaining (things and goals): waxing and full moons.

Omens: full moon.

Overcoming: waning moon.

Peace (to end hostility, war): waning moon.

Power: waxing and full moons.

Prophetic Dreams: full moon.

Protection: waxing moon.

Psychic Powers (developing, strengthening): full moon.

Quests: new moon.

Real Estate (to buy): waxing moon

Real Estate (to sell): waning moon.

Sexual Desires (to stimulate, increase): waxing moon.

Shapeshifting: full moon.

Spirit Conjurations: full moon.

Strength: waxing moon.

Teaching: waxing and full moons.

Transformations: full moon.

Travel: waxing moon.

Unions (marriages, business partnerships): waxing and full moons.

Weatherworkings (to bring forth): waxing moon.

Weatherworkings (to quell): waning moon.

Weight Gain: waxing moon.

Weight Loss: waning moon.

Wisdom (to increase): waxing and full moons.

Wish-magick: waxing and full moons.

THE MONTHS AND THE LUNAR PHASES

November ~ Snow Moon: Plan for a ritual to work on ridding yourself of negative thoughts and vibrations.

December ~ Oak Moon: Plan for a ritual to help you remain steadfast in your convictions.

January ~ Wolf Moon: Plan a ritual of protection around your home and family.

February ~ Storm Moon: Plan a ritual to ask the Old Ones for help in planning your future.

March ~ Chaste Moon: Plan a ritual to help fulfill your wishes is appropriate.

April ~ Seed Moon: Plan a ritual to physically plant your seeds of desire in Mother Earth.

May ~ Hare Moon: Plan a ritual to reaffirm your goals.

June ~ Dyad Moon: Plan a ritual to balance your spiritual and physical desires.

July ~ Mead Moon: Plan a ritual to decide what you will do once your goals have been met.

August ~ Wort Moon: Plan a ritual to preserve what you already have.

September ~ Barley Moon: Plan a ritual of Thanksgiving for all the Old Ones have given you.

October ~ Blood Moon: Plan a ritual to remember those who have passed from this world, and be sure to make an offering to them.

WEATHER SPELLS

Controlling the weather takes a lot of magic power. There are usually no negative consequences from casting a spell incorrectly, but you may need to cast the spell several times before any effect can be seen. It is not uncommon for even an experienced magic caster to fail at these spells.

To Stop the Rain

This is a spell to stop rain from coming to a town right before it falls.

When it starts getting dark, chant:

"Gods of power, Gods of might,
I bid you now, stop this plight,
Stop the rain, we need no more,
Let it fall, nevermore."

Make sure to place a lot of feeling in stopping rain from falling from the clouds and it will not fall, it will simply move to a area away from where you are and then fall. I use this all the time when I am mowing the lawn and its about to rain, then i cast this and finish the lawn.

To Make Rain Appear I

Say this outside staring at clouds above:

> *"Ancient Gods and Goddesses,*
> *I invoke thee.*
> *Waters from the sky,*
> *Let it be."*

> *"I command thee now,*
> *to thee all.*
> *Listen to my desire,*
> *Rain fall!"*

To Make Rain Appear II

The next time its raining, save some rain water in a clean vessel

Go to an open space.

Sit down in a comfortable position (preferably with a straight back).

Put the saved rain water in a bowl in front of you.
Now, start meditating. Breath in slowly and count Breath out slowly repeat a few times This is meant to calm you down and slower your breathing process. This wil help you to achieve the needed trance.

Clear out all your thoughts till you have a blank mind. Slowly (with eyes closed) put your right palm in the rain water. Close your hand into a fist (tight) then pull it out and release. Let the drops fall like a shower.

While doing this imagine that rain is pouring from the dark night in your created world inside your mind. Imagine you can hear it drop, feel and smell the damp air.

Chant:

> *Rain fall Rain Fall,*
> *From the divine sky*
> *Wet the earth, the air, the soul,*
> *leave nothing dry.*
>
> *This is my wish and pray to be*
> *I call upon thee...*
> *So moot it be!*

Calling the Wind

Calling the power of the wind is a great way to get that extra energy for your spells.

The whole intention of calling the wind is an ancient and classical one which dates before the Greeks. Many spells and rituals can be assisted by calling the wind before starting. Once you have gathered the needed items for your spell and cast your circle, turn to the north and say:

> *"Wind of the north, of cold and might*
> *Aid me in my work tonight"*

Winds from the North

The Winds that blow from the North are the cold ones. These winds are associated with level headedness. So use this time to practice spellwork for financial management, and organization.

Turn to the east and say:

> *"Wind of the east, of minds so bright*
> *Aid me in my work tonight"*

Winds from the East

Winds that blow from the East are associated with transformation, and new beginnings. When the easterly winds blow, use this time to practice spellwork involving all things new. It is also a time to write new spells, create a new ritual, or find new avenues in your chosen path.

Turn to the south and say:

> *"Wind of the south, of passion so true*
> *Aid me in my work to do"*

Winds from the South

Winds that blow from the south are commonly associated with spells for love, lust and passion. South winds give us vitality, and spellwork for banishing jealousy and selfishness from the self should be performed during this time.

Turn to the west and say:

> *"Wind of the west, so gentle and blue*
> *Aid me in my work to do"*

Winds from the West

Winds that blow from the west are associated with healing. During these winds practice cleansing and healing rituals. Intuition in the natural Witch is strong during these winds, so take advantage of this and practice spellwork, which involves using your inner strength to its capacity.

The power of the winds powers can give tremendous intensity to your magick. Depending on which wind is blowing, vibrations on the earth will differ.

If you hang a ribbon to a tree or fence, you will be able to see which wind is blowing; this will be the wind you will announce your intentions to as you perform the spell.

When invoking the winds for spellwork, you will need to be outside.

Snow Day Spell

Items:

1 black Candle

Directions:
Light the candle the night before the day you want the snowday. Then recite this 3 times:

> *"Goddess Hecate,*
> *I call upon thee,*
> *make tomorrow a snowday,*
> *so mote it be"*

Note: This spell must be used to catch up on work, or something important, not to be used for unimportant things or it will either not work, or backfire.

Must use new candle every time.

Spell for a Sunny day or Clear Skies

Take a container of some kind (any kind will do) and pour some water into it, preferably mineral water or spring water. Then put some salt in it and leave it on a windowsill if it is sunny or windy (if windy you need to make sure that it is secured and wont blow away). If it is wet outside or humid and the water will not evaporate away, leave it in your house in a warm place or by a window.

As you pour the salt in, imagine the mixture becoming the clouds in the sky visualize it evaporating and the clouds evaporating with it.

Then leave it to evaporate in its place.
Only remove when all of the water has gone.

INCENSE

Incense can be the best way to infuse earth energy into your workings with fire. It is a way to engage in aromatherapy, earth energy, and fire energy all at the same time. Incense can be extremely useful in magickal workings, and just to have in the home in order to purify or sweeten the energy of a space. Though such a purification isn't usually necessary, it can really help the practitioner get in the right state of focus. The herbs and scents used in incense should be chosen carefully. When the incense burns, the energies of the burning or smoldering herbs and various ingredients alter the energy of the room or space. It is important to have it altered in the right manner. If you are burning incense or a scented candle merely to sweeten the smell of a place, choosing a scent that is merely aesthetically pleasing to you is fine.

HOW IS INCENSE MADE?

Incenses are composed of a variety of leaves, flowers, roots, barks, woods, resins, and oils, usually mixed with some form of gunpowder or salt peter to keep the fire smoldering. There are some very common herbs and oils that can be easily kept around the house so that you can

make incense whenever you wish. Handy ingredients
would include:

Frankincense
Rose petals
Bay
Cloves
Cinnamon
Sandalwood
Basil
Rosemary
Cedar

Remember that a substance may smell very different when
it is burning. Think of tobacco—raw tobacco is very sweet,
but when burned, quickly takes on an acrid, bitter smell.

There are two main kinds of incense—combustible and not
combustible. Combustible incense can be burned in the
form cones and sticks, whereas noncumbustible incense
must be sprinkled onto glowing charcoal to release its
fragrance. Both are fairly easy to make at home.

A note about safety: incense can cause a fire if left
unattended. If you routinely work with candles and
incense, make sure that there is no long fabric or drapes or

anything flammable that could possibly fall on or in the flame. It's also a good idea to have a fire extinguisher handy, or, at the very least, a large bowl of water nearby so that you can take action if things go wrong. Never let pets or children wander around near fire or incense unless you are watching closely. Thousands of homes burn down every year because of candles, smoldering cigarettes, and incense. It can happen to you, too, if you're not careful!

That said, responsible use of fire, candles, and incense can be a great addition to any home, magickal or non magickal. Though making your own incense is time consuming, messy, and kind of a pain given that it can be purchased so cheaply, some feel that there is a certain satisfaction in hand-picking the ingredients and making the scents at home. Personally, I would love to make my own incense but since there are so many hours in the day, I just buy mine. Purists, however, may want to make their own. So, moving on to making incense...

NONCONBUSTIBLE INCENSE

This is the easiest to make by far, so you may want to get started with noncombustible before venturing into creating combustible incense. Before you start, make sure that each ingredient has been ground very finely. You can use a mortar and pestle, or a rolling pin, or a special electric grinder reserved for incense making.

When everything has been ground, take a large wooden or ceramic bowl and mix the resins and gums together with your hands.

Next, mix in all the powdered leaves, barks, flowers and roots
 Now add any oils or liquids that are included in the recipe.

Charge and empower the incense and it is done.

Store in a tightly capped jar. Label carefully, including the name of the incense and date of composition.

COMBUSTIBLE INCENSE

Combustible incense requires gum tragacanth glue or mucilage so that the powder will stick enough to be made into a cone, or adhered to a small piece of wood. To make tragacanth glue, place a teaspoon of ground tragacanth in a cup of warm water. Whisk it and take away the foam or froth that results with a spoon.

Let the tragacanth absorb the water until it becomes a thick, bitter-smelling paste. Sticks are hard to make, but if you decide to try, the mucilage should be thin. For blocks and cones a thicker mucilage should be made.

If you can't find tragacanth, try using gum arabic in its place. After you have mixed whatever adhesive you will be using, set it aside to cool. If it gets too viscous, add more warm water and stir it a little.

To make the base of the cone incense, whatever the fragrance, you'll need:

6 parts ground Charcoal (not self-igniting),

1 part ground Benzoin,

2 parts ground Sandalwood,

1 part ground Orris root

6 drops essential oil

2 to 4 parts mixed, incense from one of the below recipes

Mix the first four ingredients until all are well blended. Add the drops of essential oil and mix again with you hands. You can put it in a grinder if you want, just to make sure the particles are fine enough. Then add the incense.

Then using a small kitchen scale, weigh the completed incense and add ten percent potassium nitrate. Mix this until the white powder is thoroughly blended. Next, add the trag glue, slowly, and mix with your hands. For cone incense you'll need a very stiff, dough-like texture.

On a piece of waxed paper, shape the mixture into basic cone shapes,. When you've made up your cone incense, let it dry for two to seven days in a warm place. Your incense is finished.

INCENSE RECIPES

Aloe and Clove Incense

2 parts Myrrh

1 part Wood Aloe

a few drops clove oil

Burn to contact spirits during rituals or as a simple consecration incense.

Winter Incense

4 parts Benzoin

2 parts Gum Mastic

1 part Violet

1 pinch Wormwood

1 pinch Mistletoe

Burn to invoke the powers of the element of Air

Altar Incense

3 parts Frankincense

2 parts Myrrh

1 part Sage

Burn as a general incense on the altar to purify the area.

Venus Incense

1 part Cinnamon or Clove

1 part Sandalwood

Few drops Cypress or Pine oil

Burn during rituals designed to attract love.

Apollo Incense

4 parts Frankincense

2 parts Myrrh

2 parts Cinnamon

1 part Rosemary

Burn during divination rituals.

IX. WORKING WITH THE ELEMENTS:
Some Last Thoughts

When ever possible, hold the rites in sacred places such as forests, seashores, mountain tops, desert plains, or near a tranquil lake or river. If you can not do this, a garden or inner chamber is fine. Make sure that it is prepared in advance with fumes, flowers and ornamentation.

Seek out wisdom from natural things (from the elements), but also from books, poems and rare writings. Most people prepare for a ritual by cleansing themselves both physically and psychically. This can be an actual bath or a hand bath to cleanse away mundane thoughts and worries and prepare mentally for ritual. You can bless the water with the four elements and/or add magical to the bath.

Do not just grab any stick of incense for your Circle. Know what is in it, and know the magical significance of each ingredient. Benson's, "Herbalism- A Complete Reference Guide to Frequently used Magickal Herbs and Spices", and "Potions, Herbs, Oils & Brews" or Cunningham's, "Incense, Oils and Brews" are good sources for incense recipes..

NOTES:

NOTES:

NOTES:

NOTES:

www.ingramcontent.com/pod-product-compliance
Lightning Source LLC
Chambersburg PA
CBHW022023090426
42739CB00006BA/257